Modern Curriculum Press
**BEGINNING
TO
READ**
Series

Library of Congress Cataloging in Publication Data

McLenighan, Valjean.
    Know when to stop.

    SUMMARY: Retells the fate of the fisherman's greedy wife who was never satisfied with the wishes granted her by an enchanted fish.
    [1. Fairy tales. 2. Folklore—Germany] I. Haesly, Jack. II. Title.
PZ8.M1758Kn   398.2'0943 [E]   79-24520

Library of Congress Catalog Card Number: 79-24520

ISBN 0-8136-5083-6 (Hardbound)
ISBN 0-8136-5583-8 (Paperback)
89
123456789

Know When to Stop

Valjean McLenighan

Illustrated by Jack Haesly

MODERN CURRICULUM PRESS
CLEVELAND · TORONTO

5

7

8

16

17

18

Three days go by...

Hello, my pet.

Do not give me that.
Look at this house.
It is too little.
I want something big.
And I want some helpers.

20

Oh, well.

Fish, oh, fish.
Down in the blue.
Come here fast.
I have something to ask.

What can I
do for you?

The Mrs. wants a big house now.
And she wants some helpers.

She can have them.
They will be there
when you get back.
But know when to stop.

ZAP

22

25

27

28

30

31

Valjean McLenighan is a writer, editor, and producer.

Know When to Stop uses the 100 words listed below.

a	get	make	talks
about	give	man	tell
ahead	go	me	thank
all	good	Mrs.	that
am	got	much	the
and		my	them
are	happy		there
ask	have	new	thing
at	he	no	this
	hello	not	three
back	helpers	now	to
bad	her		too
be	here	oh	
better	him	on	up
big	house	one	
blue	how		very
but		pet	
	I	put	want(s)
day(s)	in		was
did	is	run	way
do	it		we
down		said	well
	jump	say	what
eat		see	when
	know	she	where
fast		show	will
find	let	so	
fish	like	some	you
for	little	something	
	look	stop	
		story	